To MIKE.
Happy Birthday
2002.
Doug.

To MIKE.

Happy Birthday
2002.

EDINBURGH

THE PHOTOGRAPHIC ATLAS

getmapping.com + HarperCollins*Publishers*

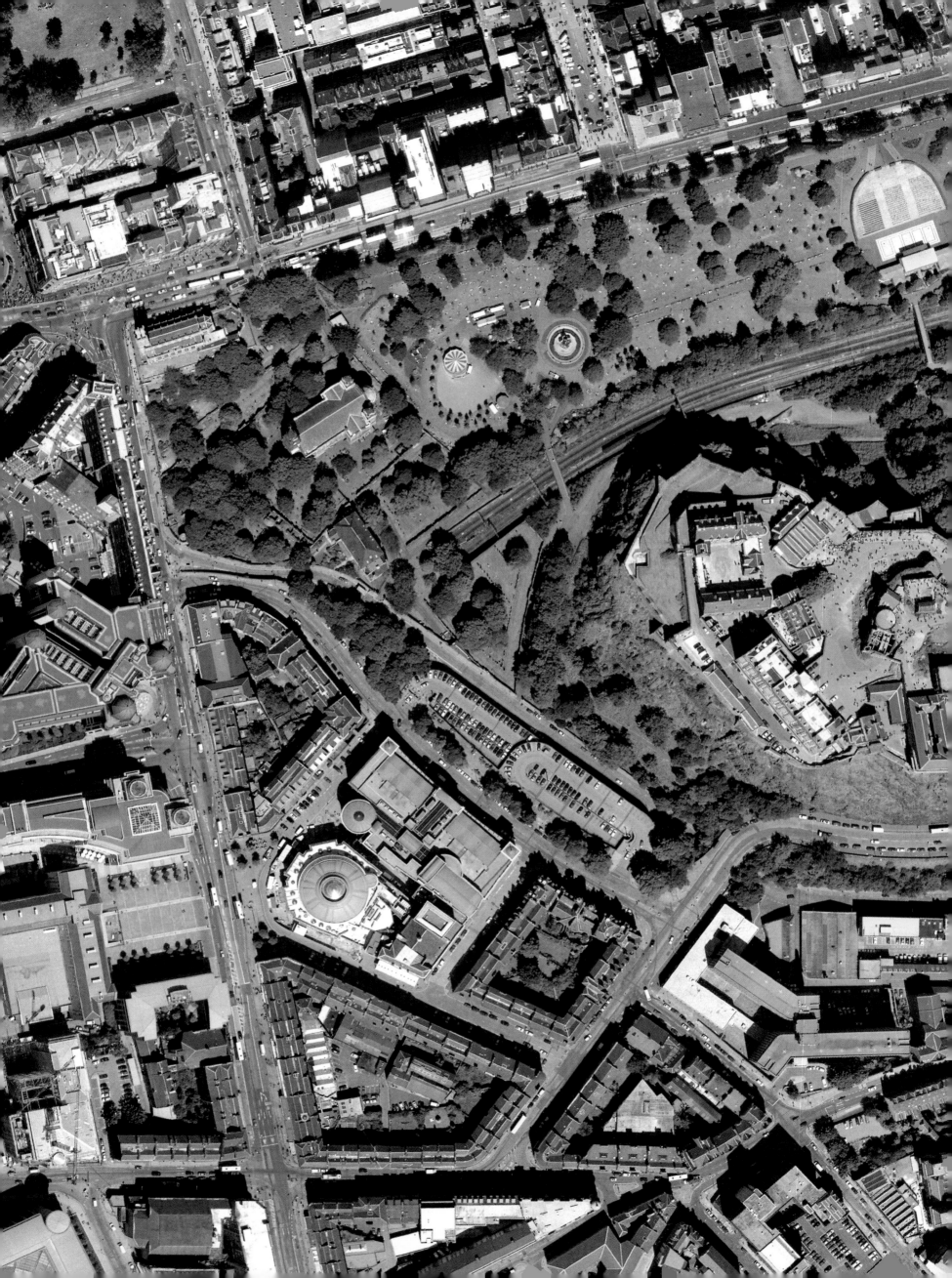

First published in 2001 by
HarperCollinsPublishers
77–85 Fulham Palace Road
London W6 8JB

The HarperCollins website address is
www.**fire**and**water**.com

Photography © 2001 Getmapping.com plc/The XYZ Digital Map Company (www.xyzmaps.com)
Cartography © 2001 HarperCollinsPublishers Ltd

Getmapping.com plc hereby asserts its moral right to be identified as the author of this work.

Getmapping can produce an individual print of any area shown in this book, or of any area
within the United Kingdom. The image can be centred wherever you choose, printed at any size
from A6 to 7.5 metres square, and at any scale up to 1:1,000. For further information, please
contact Getmapping on 01530 835685, or log on to www.getmapping.com

Pages 72–79 are based upon the Ordnance Survey Mapping with the permission of
The Controller of Her Majesty's Stationery Office © Crown Copyright 100018598

A CIP catalogue record for this book is available from the British Library.

ISBN: 0 00 712278 0

05 04 03 02 01
9 8 7 6 5 4 3 2 1

Book design by SMITH

Colour origination by Colourscan, Singapore
Printed and bound in Great Britain by Bath Press Colourbooks

contents

The key to photography on page 10 indicates complete area of coverage
The corresponding cartography page reference is located at the bottom left of each spread
The photography and the cartography share the same standard grid system
The grid interval is 500 metres for the photography (pages 12–71) and 1 kilometre for the cartography (pages 72–80)

newhaven
54/55

leith docks

56/57

leith

trinity
16/17

broughton
pilrig
south leith
18/19

seafield

58/59

restalrig
craigentinny
24/25
26/27
abbeyhill
meadowbank

portobello

princes street
gardens
32/33
34/35
willowbrae

holyrood park
arthur's seat
62/63
duddingston

the meadows
40/41
42/43

grange
newington
niddrie
prestonfield
48/49
50/51
craigmillar

68/69

66/67
inneredun

braid hills
liberton
danderhall

70/71

gilmerton

53

54

14

21

54

13

22

16

Scale 1:3,000 see cartography pages 74/75

56

18

57

2

58

27

12

53/61

M

28

14

15

21

30

24

23

18

31

40

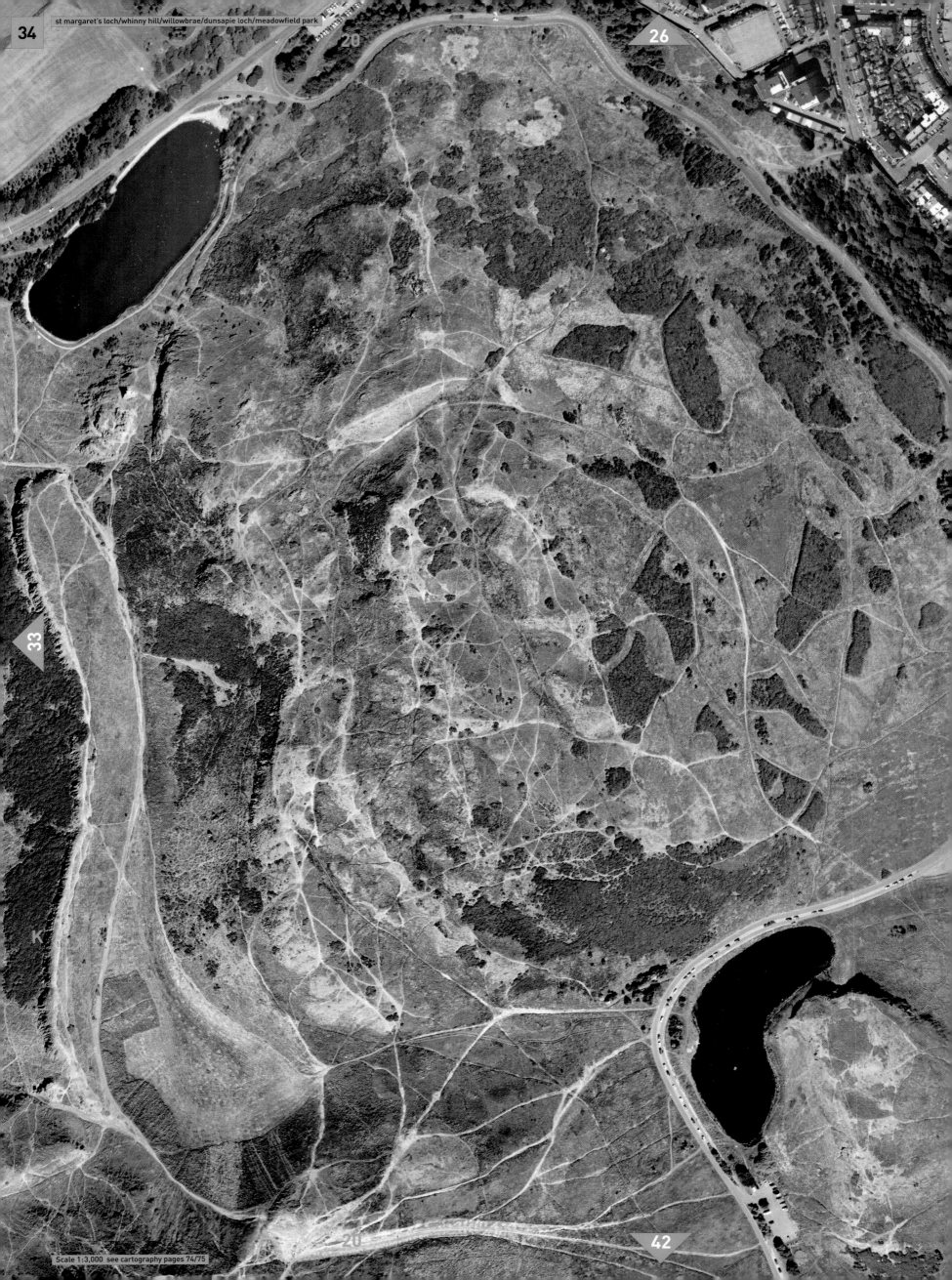

20

26

33

K

42

20

27

22

62

43

37

46

40

39

34

41

36

12

61/65

G

65

12

45

Scale 1:3,000 see cartography pages 78/79

47

Scale 1:3,000 see cartography pages 78/79

67

69

54

13

21

T

S

53

54

T

S

56

55

17/8

20

T

S

R

Q

19

27

25

Scale 1:6,000 see cartography pages 74/75

P

O

N

M

53
61
21
29
37
45

59 27 28

L

K

J

I

69 28

45

65

51

H

G

F

67

25

Scale 1:6,000 see cartography pages 78/79

F

E

23

24

68

25

67

25

24

69

26

28

D

C

A

26

27

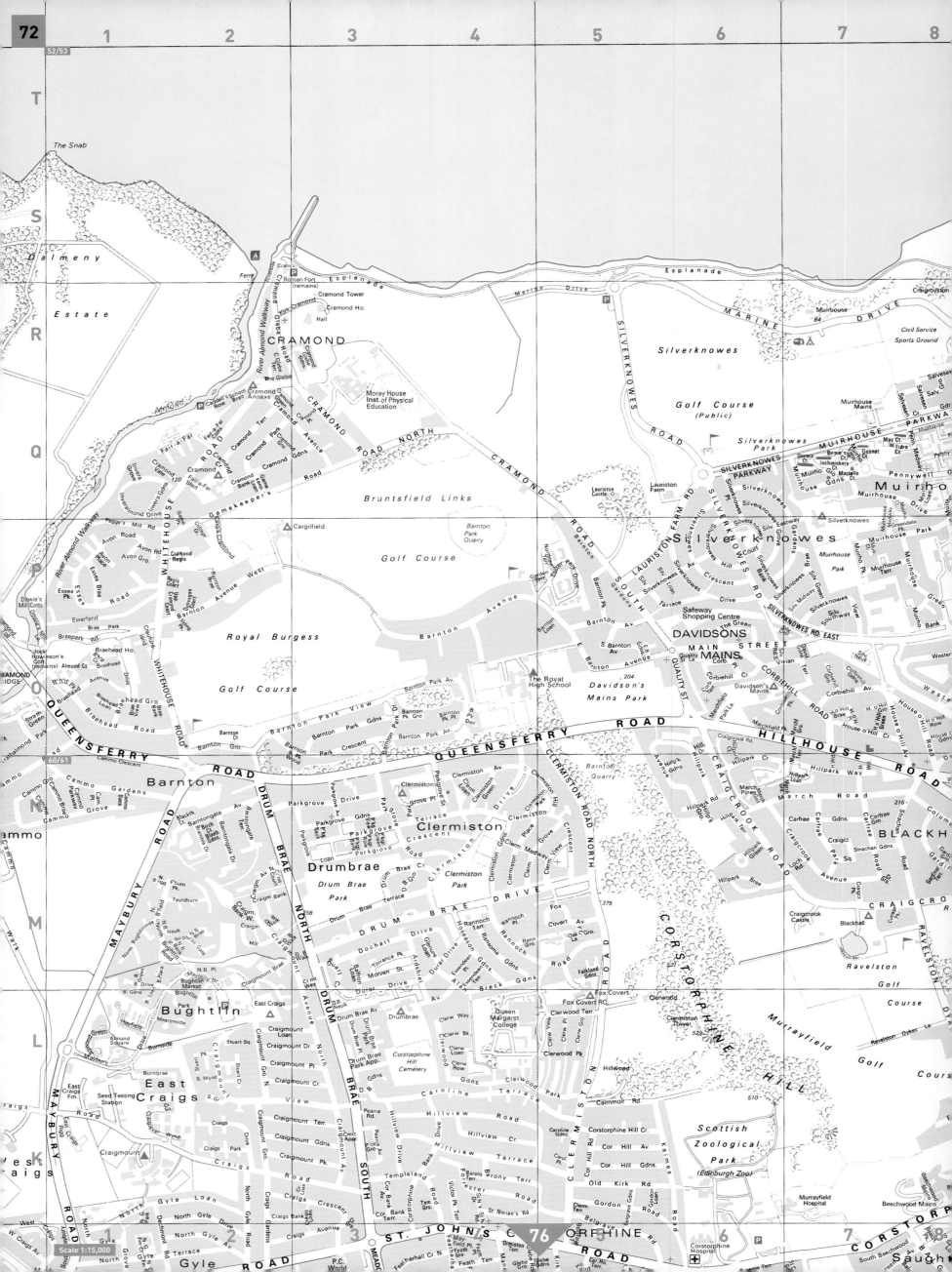